The Os of the Wild Woosi

of the

by Lisa Woosi Wildwood

For my partners,
LightFoot McBride
and Emily Siskin,
and my community,
who have embraced my
Os like no others...

Table of Contents

Foreplay 1

Now Please! 2

Yes! Yes! Yes! 3

The Os of the Wild Woosi........ 5

"You can't wait for orgasm. You have to go after it with a vibrator."

◊

The Wild Woosi's warped version of a Jack London quote

Foreplay

You know, I never used to think much about orgasms. I liked them, to be sure. I liked thinking up new ways to draw out orgasms. I was very inventive...when I was alone.

Do you ever worry with a partner, especially a new partner? I worried...about having or not having an orgasm... about what my face looked like when I was coming...about inconveniencing my lover or boring him...about taking too long to come. Any sigh or change of position... it makes you worry more. In my mind, I imagined my lover thinking "hurry up woman!"

My orgasm, if it ever did come, waited a very long time to get there. I sometimes felt that I had to come before my lover could come. Somewhere I'd heard that it's impolite for a guy to come first. Now his orgasm is dependent on mine...Oh No!

There was also only one orgasm. Some people call it "The Big-O." I either had The Big-O or I didn't. And with a lover, I always felt kind of inadequate if I didn't have one, and worried (that word again) that he would believe it was because he wasn't a good enough lover, or worse, I was just not orgasmic. (Frigid!)

Now Please!

"I am orgasmic!" I would think. "I can come in 5 minutes!" Really! ... In a room all by myself, I can.

Don't ask me to prove it, though. Anyone watching and the worries start up and my orgasm would play hard-to-get.

Then one of my lovers and I started talking about the definition of orgasm. Why was only the Big-O called an orgasm? And what were those little waves of pleasure I get that make my whole body shudder, the ones that build and build and build until The Big-O? Why can't those be

Little-Os?   And if those are Os, well then, I have lots and lots of Os....   I was multi-orgasmic!... Or was I? ...

I resisted at first. After all, I'd lived most of my life believing there was only one O. One specific definition, one way of having one. I'd hear of woman who were multi-orgasmic and think...surely I would pass out.

Resistance is futile though... once I started thinking about orgasms, I was compelled to embrace them all. I went from feeling self-conscious about having "The O" to celebrating Os in whatever form they came. I am no longer confined to one type of O... I am free to have as many orgasms as I desire! And you are too!

Yes! Yes! Yes!

In an orgasm-rich world, what's with "Big-O" and "Little-O"? How limiting and downright un-orgasmic are those names!

~3~

So began my quest to classify orgasms. To name them and acknowledge them and thereby allow myself to orgasm as much and in any sort of way I choose.

In sharing these with you, I invite you to embrace all of your Os! Throw off the chains of Big-O oppression! You too can be multi-orgasmic!

◊

Please collect your safer-sex supplies before proceeding...

◊

The Os

of the

Wild Woosi

◊

Ready? Steady... O!

◊

Cheerio

◊

Screaming, body-twitching O
(formerly known as the Big-O)

Petito

◊

Little wave of pleasure building up
to a Cheerio

Spaghetti-o

◊

Being touched by his noodly
appendage

Akimbo

◊

O while trying one of the leg-twisting positions in the Kama Sutra

Mambo

◊

O number 5

Alterego

◊

WTF? What was that? I didn't know I could be like that! Can we do that again?

Vibrato

◊

o by violin

Potato

◊

An O that satisfies you for a long time (sticks to your ribs...)

Amino

◊

The fundamental building block
of all Os

Kinko

◊

Any O during kinky play

Marco Polo

◊

Feeling around in the dark,
calling for your O

Rodeo

◊

Any O had while you're tied up in any way, especially hog-tied. One of the many types of Kinkos

Bandito

◊

Secretly using another person or
object to help you 0 without their
knowledge or consent

Bilbo

◊

A Petito before Breakfast, then a
Cheerio before Second Breakfast,
two Rodeos just before Elevenses,
just a little taste of a Potato before
Luncheon, and then free-for-all
O's anytime between Afternoon
Tea and Supper, supplemented
with plenty of kisses in between

Alamo

◊

Laying siege to an O

Biblio

◊

O of Biblical proportions

Bongo

◊

◯ gyrating to a drum beat

Diablo

◊

Every time you have an O, god
kills a kitten

Brillo

◊

The ecstasy obtained by a really
good back scratch

Calypso

◊

Being tempted into having an O
by a beautiful seductress who then
leaves you stranded

Cameo

◊

A brief appearance by a well-known O

Amontillado

◊

Plotting to give your ex an amazing O after they've broken up with you, just to show them how good it would have been if they'd stayed with you

Cheeto

◊

Fake O. Please... don't go there!

Topo

◊

O while tracing the contours of
your lover...

Volvo

◊

Safe, upper-middle-class O

Cinco de Mayo

◊

An O that sets you free

Commando

◊

When you're ordered to have an O.
Can be a kinko

Ammo

◊

Rapid-fire Os

Camo

◊

Doing it quietly while hiding in
the bushes, trying to make sure
no-one sees you

G.I. Joe

◊

Having Commando Ammos in Camo

Crypto

◊

Refusing to provide any sort of
feedback to your partner so they
have to unravel the mystery of
how to make you O through their
amazing powers of deduction and
ESP

Harpo

◊

Being nagged into having an O.
Next to impossible to achieve

Bacterio

◊

The oops-I-should-have-used-a-condom O

Dayglo

◊

Having such a good O that you're
still beaming the next morning

Demo

◊

Showing someone exactly how you
like to be made to O

Armadillo

◊

Prying your way past
insecurities, ticklishness, and
baggage to finally find that soft
spot where you can O

Churro

◊

◊ using a toy that's "ribbed for
your pleasure"

Preggo

◊

The she-said-she-was-on-the-pill O

Ditto

◊

Trying to copy how someone else
had an O

Innuendo

◊

Hinting that you want an O

Dodo

◊

O that makes you stumble
around, momentarily stupified

Pluto

◊

Thought it was an O, but it was
just too small

Maraschino

◊

Pretending you still have your
cherry to get an O

Dynamo

◊

Having one O right after the other,
such that your lover contemplates
hooking you up to the electric grid

Echo

◊

Aftershock O

Garbo

◊

An O that makes you "just want
to be alone"

Double-O

◊

An O that occurs while
transmitting a message in Morse
Code through the genitals as
you're tied together in dire straits
by the evil Blofeld

Grotto

◊

Going down in the dark under the
covers and giving an O that echoes

Dildo

◊

Self-explanatory...

Isn't it?

Well, if it isn't to you, then get
yourself down to your nearest
high-quality sexual toy store and
ask them for one...

Halo

◊

Immaculate O

Gung Ho

◊

O with the whole platoon

Pinocchio

◊

Lying about having an O

Heigh-ho

◊

O with seven dwarves. One of many types of kinkos

Imbroglio

◊

An O that occurs in a puppy pile
and you're not quite sure who gave
it to you —very rare.

.

Maestro

◊

A well-orchestrated O

Virtuoso

◊

O in a white dress, all the while protesting that you really shouldn't be doing this...

Curio

◊

What happens when I do this....
oooo...ahhhh

Tornado

◊

O that leaves your head spinning
and the sheets flung across the
room

Manifesto

◊

Delivering a detailed directive on
exactly how you expect to be made
to O

Credo

◊

An O that is freely asked, freely
given, freely taken or freely
tossed! (The credo of all Os for the
Wild Woosi!)

Merino

◊

O assisted by wool, either attached
to the sheep or unattached (can be
a kinko, or not)

Quasimodo

◊

Bending yourself into ridiculous
contortions to have an O, and then
limping around the next day

Mojo

◊

Be one with your O mojo and do it
for the sake of making it way
cool! (Thanks to St. Crispy)

Neutrino

◊

Small but powerful 0

NoGo

◊

The little O that couldn't

Oh No

◊

The she-said-she-was-18 O

Soprano

◊

An O that makes you sing

Duo

◊

Simultaneous sopranos

Typo

◊

Two technical writers were lying
on a trampoline... (don't ask :)

Mango

◊

When you're perfectly ripe for
having an O

Patio

◊

O while being spanked. One of
many kinkos

Waldo

◊

Trying, with no hints, to find the exact spot to make someone else O

Placebo

◊

You think you had an O, but it
really wasn't

Gogo

◊

After one O, you're ready for the next. Like an ammo, but drop the guns and add pink boots and a psychadelic dress

Albino

◊

Vanilla O

Portfolio

◊

Trying to impress someone by
bragging about your ability to
give others 0s

Hawaii 5-O

◊

O that gets you booked

Marshmallow

I want s'more please!

Promo

◊

Giving your boss an O to get a head

Roger Wilco

◊

We are a go for an O. Roger that

Motto

◊

O that causes you to scream something repeatedly, like:

"Oh Yes Oh Yes"

"Oh god oh god oh god"

"Now please Now please"

Add your O motto here:

_____

Solo

◊

Masturbating O

Hero

◊

O that saves you

So-n-So

(usually preceded by "That Old")

◊

Anyone who refuses to give you
an O

So-so

◊

Doesn't happen, no such thing
exists...

Logo

◊

Corporate-approved O

Taco

◊

Help, I'm O'ing and I can't shut
up!

Amigo

◊

A real friend is a friend who helps
you have an O

Telephoto

◊

A heart-stopping look from a
stranger across the room that
makes you come a little

Sympatico

◊

Having a spontaneous O while watching someone else O

Iago

◊

Being evilly manipulated into
having an O

Americano

◊

I want YOU to have an O!

Torpedo

◊

An O given when your lover's
submarine locks onto your target

UFO

◊

Unidentified Future O.

Bravo

◊

An O that's so loud that your
roommates hear and come to
applaud you

Video

◊

O had while trying to copy what
they're doing in a porn movie

Casino

◊

Having an O when you figured
the odds were against it

Visio

◊

A flow diagram documenting
your stages of arousal ultimately
leading to an O

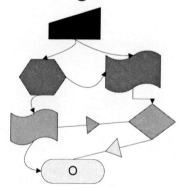

Bravado

◊

Bragging about how amazing
your Os are

Yo-Yo

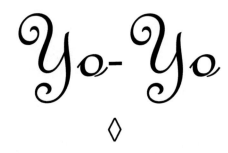

I'm coming... I'm coming!

Oh faster! Faster!...

Oh yes! I'm coming... I'm coming!

Oh no... slower...

Oh Yes! Yes! Yes!

Techno

We are the sex toys...
resistance is futile...
you will be stimulated...

Zero

◊

No 0 -- I don't want to talk about
it

Thank You!

I would like to thank the following people
who have given me orgasms:

LightFoot	Kyrie	Richard
Emily	Aylea	Judy
Barbara	Ken	Elon
Mike	John	David
Chris Bickle	Tom	JB
Eugene	Autumn	Don
Jean	Butterfly	Tree
Kelly	Tamara	Marcus
Marvin	Moonstorm	Randy
St. Crispy	Angi	Rob

She-who-must-not-be-embarrassed   :-o

For more Os, see
www.wildwoosi.com.

This page intentionally left blank . . .

(for you to add some more Os)